VOLTAIRE

A Life from Beginning to End

Table of Contents

Introduction

In defiance of his father's wishes, who wanted a lawyer in the family, Voltaire became a writer and playwright. Defiance came as naturally to him as breathing. For as long as anyone could remember, kings and church had determined humankind's thoughts and behavior. Voltaire, along with other Enlightenment writers, would change that. His antipathy toward the privileges of the aristocracy and the dogma of the Catholic Church had him imprisoned twice in the Bastille and eventually forced him into exile. Voltaire was the bane of every well-born aristocrat he met because he refused to grant anyone special dignity due to an accident of birth. He insisted that everyone deserved to be treated equally, a revolutionary idea at the time.

When it came to the aristocratic elite, Voltaire used his words like a sword to inflict deep wounds. His insistence that matters of religion, even the existence of God, should be questioned caused his writings to be banned and burned in many countries. But he never stopped writing. His works have survived as some of the most important of the European Enlightenment.

It wasn't until later in life that Voltaire turned some of his abstract ideas into concrete action. He began to financially help those impoverished by government taxation. He also worked hard at exposing the unfairness of the French legal system, which could accuse and sentence a man to die without providing due cause. Voltaire held up a mirror to a society that took aristocratic and legal privileges for the rich for granted. For that, he was loudly denounced.

Ultimately, Voltaire lived a productive life by his own rules. He taught his readers that they could do likewise.

Chapter One

The Enlightenment: When the World Changed

"Man is free at the instant he wants to be."

—Voltaire

Voltaire was born under the name François-Marie Arouet on November 21, 1694, in Paris, France. His father, François Arouet, was a minor government official, and his mother, Marie Marguerite Daumard, came from a lesser noble family. The family wasn't rich, but they were comfortable.

Voltaire was a man born at the right time. Following centuries of religious strife in Europe and the continuing belief in the absolute power of the monarchy and the church, thinkers of the Age of Enlightenment were questioning the basis of human rights at every level. The discovery of the New World, the spread of the Reformed Protestant religion, and new inventions in science were all bringing about a revolution in politics and society as a whole. It was a time when anything seemed possible.

The settlement of America was greatly influenced by Enlightenment thinker John Locke, who was to have a major influence on Voltaire. It was Locke who made some shocking assertions about natural law that no one had previously considered. Before the Enlightenment, everyone's fate was established at birth. If you were born a royal, you were destined to rule. If you came from a farming family, you would likely spend your life reaping and sowing. Kings and popes ruled over all individuals, and even they were answerable to God. The government and the church where at the apex of everyone's lives.

Then along came John Locke, who insisted that everyone had natural rights that neither king nor God could take away. People had a right to challenge their rulers. People had a right to question a God who could predetermine men's destiny. These ideas may not be radical in modern times, but when Voltaire was growing up, they could not have been more shocking. Enlightenment thinkers strove to unshackle the minds of men. Men had a right to think for themselves! This was considered heresy.

In the prior century, thousands of people had been killed at the stake for daring to assert their own religious beliefs. Pre-Enlightenment, people were at the mercy of an angry God. Kings demanded absolute obedience. Thinkers such as Voltaire challenged the idea that humankind was predestined to misery. There was not one group of Enlightenment thinkers. Philosophers from America, England, France, and other countries wrote about various new approaches to life. They may have disagreed on details, but they all demanded that old ideas be challenged. Curiosity was to be pursued at all cost.

Voltaire was born during the end of the reign of King Louis XIV, the Sun King who'd declared himself to be the absolute ruler of his domain and every person in it when he said, "*L'état, c'est moi!* (I am the state!)". As Voltaire was growing up, faith and subservience were losing its grip on the population as reason and facts grew in importance. For most of its history, humankind had submitted to authority, be it church or state. Voltaire was one of the Enlightenment thinkers determined to change the way people thought and acted. But before he could do that, he would need to get over the first hurdle on his way to freedom: his father.

Voltaire's mother had died when he was young, and he and his father were frequently at odds. Mr. Arouet insisted the boy become a lawyer and sent him to a strict Jesuit school for a classical education. A white-collar profession, however, never held any interest for Voltaire. Even at a young age, Voltaire knew he wanted to be a writer. Mr. Arouet attempted, unsuccessfully, to interest his recalcitrant son in a position at court. He even tried bribery. Voltaire refused. He did, however, accept the position of secretary to the French ambassador in The Hague in 1713. There, he became enmeshed in an affair with a high official's daughter. The ambassador immediately discharged Voltaire from his duties and sent him back to Paris. It was the beginning of a lifetime of conflicts Voltaire would experience with authority.

Upon his return to Pairs, a somewhat contrite Voltaire made a try at a legal career. He gave up the idea very quickly, however, knowing that all he wanted was to write. Instead, Voltaire sought out young intellectuals in the hope of interesting them in his verses. The theater was his real goal. It was a critical place for any writer, and the only theater worthwhile was the prestigious Comédie Française in Paris. While Voltaire and his father continued to argue about his future, Voltaire was in the process of selling his first play, *Oedipus*, to the Comédie Française. He was now officially a writer.

Life in Paris held everything a young man could want. Following the death of Louis XIV and his despotic rules in 1715, under the regency of Louis XV, Paris was alive once more. Gambling and balls were all the rage again. The Society of the Temple, named after the Knights of the Templars, happily supported debauched behavior, drinking, and self-indulgence. It was at the Temple that Voltaire honed his wit and love of mockery. So well-crafted was his mockery that the regency court took note and decided to send him into exile in 1716. Surprisingly, it was Voltaire's irate father who came to the rescue and had him shipped to the countryside at the chateau of the Duke of Sully instead.

Life at the castle was not a hardship. Voltaire found a lovely mistress and had the time to revise his *Oedipus* for the Comédie Française. He remained at the chateau for six months, until the regent, Philippe II, permitted him to return to Paris. Although smart and ambitious, Voltaire was still naïve in the ways of politics. As soon as he was settled in Paris, he once again wrote verses against the regent, this time accusing him of incest. This was more than Philippe would accept, and in 1717, Voltaire ended up imprisoned in the Bastille for 11 months. Defiant as ever, he refused to complain and stated he was pleased to have a quiet place to write; it was at the Bastille that Voltaire started working on his epic poem *La Henriade*. Yet pen and paper would have been difficult to come by, and mostly, it was an unpleasant time for the rebellious young writer.

The imprisonment in Bastille caused a change in Voltaire. While he would always remain defiant, he now knew how to curtail his behavior. His release from Bastille also coincided with another milestone in his life: in June 1718, he signed his name as "Arouet de Voltaire" for the first time, turning into simply "Voltaire" by the end of the year.

Chapter Two

Literary Success and Financial Failure

"I have never made but one prayer to God, a very short one: 'O Lord make my enemies ridiculous.' And God granted it."

—Voltaire

Seven months following his release from Bastille, Voltaire was able to attend the premiere of his first play, *Oedipus*. It was an immediate success, and fame hit Voltaire instantaneously. Following the success of *Oedipus*, Philippe II even sent him a monetary gift of 675 livres. George I, the king of England, sent him a gold watch. He made 3,000 pounds in royalties, and the French courts eventually provided him with an annual pension of 2,000 pounds.

Suddenly, Voltaire was in great demand socially as everyone wanted to meet this new, exciting young writer. He had no trouble having the Comédie Française stage his next plays, and he was happy to find the time for romance with the leading ladies of the stage. But although Voltaire loved the theater, he wanted to write more than just plays. He felt he had a lot more to say. France's stringent censorship laws meant that every bit of writing had to be approved by the authorities, and permission was not easy to come by. In addition to the court official censors, the Catholic Church could make life difficult for a writer.

The answer was to publish anonymously or abroad. Voltaire went on to publish several books anonymously, denying authorship. This, of course, made collecting payment difficult, which caused him financial problems. Additionally, his next play for Comédie Française, *Artémire*, was a huge failure and had to be taken off the stage almost immediately. Voltaire's father died a very wealthy man in 1722, and the division of his fortune among his three living children should have helped Voltaire's situation. However, Mr. Arouet had never forgiven his son for refusing to enter the respectable law business and had disinherited him. Voltaire rarely spoke of his father. On those occasions when the subject arose, Voltaire merely referred to him as an authority figure. It is likely that Voltaire's anti-authoritarian nature came quite naturally as a result of his relationship—or lack of one—with his only parental figure.

Following his father's death, and perhaps due to his precarious financial situation, Voltaire developed an interest in finances and investing. His adviser was the marquis de Bernières, whom he joined in several business ventures. At the same time, he began an affair with Madame de Bernières. The marquis seemed happy to share his financial knowledge as well as his spouse, and she wasn't the only woman to share Voltaire's bed. For his trip to Holland in 1722, Voltaire acquired another mistress. In her company, Voltaire experienced first-hand Holland's religious tolerance and civil liberties, which he immediately connected to the country's financial prosperity. It was quite a change from the repressive life in France, and the atmosphere suited Voltaire's inherent dislike of authority.

While in Holland, Voltaire finished his epic poem *La Henriade* and found a printer willing to publish it. The French court, however, refused publication of the poem in France. The subject matter dealt with religious fanaticism, and France's slaughter of thousands of Protestant Huguenots was still too fresh in everyone's memory. With the help of his mistress, Madame de Bernières, Voltaire secretly printed 4,000 copies of *La Henriade* and had them distributed throughout France. Despite the censors, the critics were enthusiastic. The poem was reprinted at least 60 times during Voltaire's lifetime and firmly established his reputation as a leading poet. In the meantime, he was hard at work on his next play, *Hérode et Mariamne*.

Voltaire's financial situation still had its ups and downs. He rented rooms from Madame de Bernières in Paris but found it difficult to make the rent payments. In desperation, he started gambling. Unfortunately, he lost 2,400 pounds. By the end of 1724, he considered getting an actual job to support himself. Despite the friendly relations between Voltaire, the marquis de Bernières, and Madame de Bernières, their landlord-tenant situation caused problems when his mistress insisted on timely rent payments. Their affair came to an end when he was unable to comply. The truth was, Madame de Bernières had been a pleasant amusement, but his career would always take priority.

By 1725, the young King Louis XV was 15 years old and of marriageable age. His marriage to the Polish princess Marie Leszczyńska was a great occasion at court, and Voltaire saw an opportunity to mingle with the aristocracy and create a greater name for himself. The new queen did have *Mariamne* performed at court in October. Unfortunately, Voltaire was unable to contain his sarcastic comments about the elite, and a few weeks later, he engaged in a series of public arguments with the chevalier Guy-Auguste Rohan-Chabot, eventually challenging him to a duel. It was a bad idea. Rohan-Chabot was an aristocrat, while Voltaire was a mere writer and commoner. For the second time, Voltaire found himself imprisoned at the Bastille. This time, he promised to go to England if the authorities would release him.

Eager to rid themselves of this very public nuisance, the court agreed to his exile from France within two weeks. On May 10, 1726, Voltaire set sail for England, where a new life awaited him.

Chapter Three

Banished to England

"England has forty-two religions and only two sauces."

—Voltaire

While Voltaire had achieved a certain reputation in France, he was relatively unknown in England. *Mariamne* was his only work translated into English, and it had not been met with much acclaim on the English stage. He only had a few English acquaintances, such as Lord Bolingbroke. Ironically, Lord Bolingbroke had previously been exiled to France by King George I for his anti-religious and anti-government comments. He was allowed to return to England after bribing the king's mistress. It was Bolingbroke who introduced Voltaire to the works of Enlightenment thinkers Locke and Newton.

At the time, England was a good place to live. It was undergoing a period of great prosperity and enjoying certain freedoms of actions and beliefs which were not available in France. Where Paris overflowed with political spies and intrigue, England offered the opportunity to share new thoughts, thanks largely to the popular writings of Enlightenment writer John Locke. To Voltaire, it was the equivalent of inhaling fresh air.

Voltaire could read English quite well, but he needed to improve his ability to speak. After all, his reputation had been built around his wit. He went to live in the home of an old, wealthy friend, Everard Falkener. A successful merchant, Falkener had an extensive library, of which Voltaire availed himself. He also began to socialize frequently, joining friends for the theater and other get-togethers. Within a year, Voltaire's written English had become quite proficient, and he bragged that he could swear with the most vulgar of English lords.

Soon enough, Voltaire met with English intellectuals such as Alexander Pope and Jonathan Swift. Unfortunately, his behavior when meeting Pope was very rude, and he was never invited to the English author's home again. It seemed that Voltaire could indeed offend in several languages. He remained, however, a devoted admirer of Swift. That Swift was able to publish his bitter anti-government satires without repercussion amazed him. He knew that the same writing would have gotten any writer jailed in France.

Voltaire also became intrigued by England's political system. While France was an unquestioned and all-powerful monarchy, England had the House of Commons to keep the aristocracy in check. Voltaire recognized that the House of Lords was quickly losing power. England was close to having an actual representation of the people and a Parliament to protect civil liberties, a concept virtually unknown in France. Delighted, Voltaire wrote to a friend, "Nobody is downtrodden and nobody complains. The feet of the peasant are not tortured by wooden shoes, he eats white bread, he is well clothed, and he is not afraid to increase the number of his cattle or cover his roof with tile, lest his taxes be raised." The words were somewhat hyperbolic, but life in England was an eye-opener for Voltaire.

Religion especially fascinated him. Both France and England had lived through years of war between Catholics and Protestants. However, following the ousting of King James II in 1689, Catholics, Protestants, and even atheists lived peacefully side-by-side in England. This type of tolerance, while still new to England, did not exist in France, where the sole sanctioned religion was Catholicism. Voltaire especially enjoyed the Quakers, who worshipped as they pleased without the guidance of a priest. "O blessed land!" Voltaire exclaimed. "It there were only one religion in England, there would be danger of tyranny; if there were two, they would cut each other's throats; but there are thirty, and they live together in peace."

By early 1728, Voltaire finalized his new edition of the epic poem *La Henriade*. It sold quite well, and these earnings were warmly welcomed by Voltaire who had been scraping by in England almost penniless. Toward the end of the year, however, Voltaire appeared to have become disenchanted with England and eager to return to France. The reason behind this sudden change of heart is not known, but it is believed he got into an argument with someone. In view of what is known of Voltaire's volatile character, this version of events appears extremely likely.

Before the year was out, he decided to sail back to France even though his exile had not been lifted. Not able to return to Paris, Voltaire settled down in Dieppe where he pretended to be a traveling Englishman. Here, he spent the winter in misery, suffering from ill health and possibly depression, before moving onto Saint Germain-en-Laye, which was much closer to Paris. By April of 1729, Voltaire was finally given permission to enter Paris.

In Paris, he became reacquainted with an old friend, mathematician Charles Marie de la Condamine. La Condamine had discovered a loophole in the lottery system. Together with la Condamine and other friends, Voltaire shared half a million pounds of lottery winnings every month for a year. For the first time in his life, Voltaire didn't have to worry about money, and there was more financial luck to come. Although his father had disinherited him, a clause provided that if Voltaire could prove good conduct by the age of 35, which was his current age, he would be able to recover his share of the inheritance. A court ruled in his favor and awarded him 153,000 pounds.

With money came personal freedom. Being rich enabled Voltaire to speak out more and more against the establishment and in favor of Enlightenment ideas involving freedom. When Voltaire returned to France, he brought with him three works in progress. These were not his usual plays or poems; he was developing an avid interest in politics, especially political tyranny. His next tragedy, *Brutus*, was a clear historical rendering of abuse of power. In *Letters concerning the English Nation*, Voltaire elaborated on the religious tolerance in England and on the general freedom enjoyed by its citizens. He also wrote *History of Charles XII*, a historical work about the fearless Swedish warrior king who had battled, although unsuccessfully, with Russia's Peter the Great.

Wealthy and professionally successful, Voltaire was now about the meet one of the most important women in his life.

Chapter Four

Émilie: The Love of His Life

"I found, in 1733, a young woman who thought as I did, and who decided to spend several years in the country, cultivating her mind."

—Voltaire

Twenty-seven-year-old Émilie, marquise du Châtelet, would have been remarkable during any era. A gifted mathematician and admirer of Newton, she was certainly a match for Voltaire. Voltaire's previous amours had involved mostly married society women, but while Émilie was married, she was not known for her feminine wiles. She was far more interested in learning than in petticoats. Unusual for the times, even the Enlightenment, Émilie had been encouraged by her father to study languages, including Latin, and ancient Greek literature since childhood. She proved to be a math prodigy at an early age.

Émilie and Voltaire were introduced following Voltaire's return from England. While in exile, he had been enthralled by the new scientific discoveries, especially those made by Isaac Newton. Over dinner, he found Émilie shared his fascination. He referred to her as "that lady whom I look upon as a great man. . . . She understands

Newton, she despises superstition and in short she makes me happy." Soon enough, Voltaire moved into her country home at Cirey. It was a luxurious estate, and Voltaire enjoyed living well on champagne and excellent food. Émilie's husband, the marquis du Châtelet, was frequently absent and raised no objections to the relationship.

At Cirey, Émilie helped Voltaire write his *Elements of the Philosophy of Newton*, which would be published in 1738 in Amsterdam. This scientific work would do much to spread the discoveries made by Newton. Émilie also translated much of Newton's work into French. These two people were unusual enough to set all of Paris' tongues wagging.

While they did much serious work, Voltaire, as so often was true, found it difficult to stay out of trouble. In 1735, he worked on a satirical poem called *The Maid of Orleans,* a bawdy piece about lusty monks and soldiers endeavoring to rid one of France's national icons, Joan of Arc, of her virginity. Once again, Voltaire came to the notice of the court. When secret copies of this poem were circulated, Voltaire went into hiding from the authorities. It appears that he would escape persecution this time, however, and within a few months, he was back at Cirey with Émilie.

For a short time in 1737, the French authorities expressed some interest in seeing *Elements of the Philosophy of Newton* published in France. In the end, they concluded the new ideas were far too radical and forbade publication in France. Once again, Voltaire was silenced by censorship. It wouldn't be the last time. Just before Voltaire and Émilie were to depart for a trip to Brussels, the authorities seized his outline of *The Century of Louis XIV* and publicly burned it. Since it was favorable toward the Sun King, it was assumed, without cause, that the book would disparage the current king, Louis XV.

In 1741, Voltaire was busy with a new play, *Mahomet*, a tale which depicted Muhammad, the founder of Islam, as a fraud. He was unable to have it produced in Paris, but it was eventually staged in Lille and was a tremendous success. The play passed censorship since it was about a foreign religion and did not disparage Catholicism. When it was performed in Paris, however, it was immediately denounced as an attack on all religions.

By 1745, Voltaire was involved in an affair with his niece, Marie-Louise Mignot, the daughter of his sister and the widow of Nicolas-Charles Denis. Voltaire initially tried to keep the courtship a secret from Émilie.

Meanwhile, there was an opening at the Académie Française, an elite club of the country's top intellectuals. Voltaire was eager to be a part of this group. His first application for membership was turned down due to his well-known antipathy toward religion. For his second attempt at membership, he wrote long letters to three clergymen stating that he was of impeccable character. "I am a true citizen and a true Catholic," Voltaire asserted. When his friends learned of his obvious interest in joining this group, they mocked him severely, but he didn't care. His second application was rejected, as well. For most of his life, Voltaire remained torn between his disdain of the elite and the knowledge that he needed them in order to promote himself and his work.

Another chance to become noticed by the French court came when Voltaire was offered the job of writing the libretto for an opera about the French dauphin's marriage to the Spanish infanta called *The Princess of Navarre*. This was not an easy assignment for Voltaire since he knew little about opera, but he saw it as another chance to join the Académie Française. The opera was a splendid success, and the king, Louis XV, offered Voltaire the position of Gentleman in Ordinary as well as the King's Historian, which included an annual salary of 2,000 pounds.

Being a part of the king's inner circle proved as advantageous as Voltaire had hoped. Thanks to the prodding of the king's mistress, Madame de Pompadour, he was finally accepted into the Académie Française in 1746. By paying attendance to the king and becoming a favorite of the king's mistress, Voltaire had become a full-fledged courtier. He got what he wanted, but one wonders how he felt about the price he had to pay to get there. The truth was, this was to be the most miserable time of Voltaire's life. His health was failing; he was frequently depressed. Shifting his affections between Émilie and Marie-Louise brought him no satisfaction.

A couple of years later, Émilie met the handsome poet Jean François de Saint-Lambert and ended the sexual part of her relationship with Voltaire. Although he was upset, Voltaire agreed to remain friends. Then, in 1749, Émilie died giving birth to Saint-Lambert's child. Following her death, Voltaire would help publish her translations of Newton's work. These translations are still being used today.

Voltaire not only lost Émilie, but Marie-Louise also turned to a younger lover temporarily, sending Voltaire into a deep depression. He was alone now. Being a courtier was not what he wanted, either. In 1749, he sold his position as Gentleman in Ordinary for 60,000 pounds.

Chapter Five

Encyclopédie

"It is forbidden to kill; therefore all murderers are punished unless they kill in large numbers and to the sound of trumpets."

—Voltaire

Voltaire was now middle-aged and had spent his life trying to gain recognition. At the time, he didn't see himself as part of a movement. Voltaire was far too concerned with his own plans to pay too much attention to the world around him—unless it suited his ambitions. As a matter of fact, with the major exception of Newton, he could be rudely dismissing toward other Enlightenment thinkers.

Jean-Jacques Rousseau, two decades younger than Voltaire, was a rising member of the Enlightenment movement. In 1750, he sent Voltaire a copy of his major essays, published subsequently as *Discourse on the Arts and Sciences*. These essays helped establish Rousseau firmly within the Enlightenment movement. Voltaire, however, responded dismissively, "I am hardly in a position to read prize essays which schoolboys compose for Académie de Dijon." Voltaire was equally dismissive when Denis Diderot sent him an essay. He also refused to correspond with d'Alembert, a fan of Newton and brilliant mathematician.

In 1748, Diderot and d'Alembert began work on what was to become the systematic dictionary of the Enlightenment, known as *Encyclopédie* (in English: *Encyclopedia, or a Systematic Dictionary of the Sciences, Arts, and Crafts*). It was to undergo many revisions with many more contributors. At first, Voltaire appeared not to be aware of, or lacked any interest in, this major academic accomplishment. This encyclopedia was intended to change the way people thought and provide people with the information they needed to arrive at their own conclusions instead of relying on established dogma. It was the epitome of the Enlightenment. This massive work had 28 volumes, a total of 71,818 essays, along with thousands of illustrations.

To avoid French censorship, Diderot had the first seven volumes published in Switzerland. The *Encyclopédie* demanded proof for the existence of a God, and it demanded the right to worship as one pleased. French author André Morellet earned a period of imprisonment at Bastille after coming out in agreement with these thoughts. When it came to politics, the *Encyclopédie* shifted political power to the people, an ideal especially espoused by Rousseau. It also insisted that individuals had natural rights that were beyond the purview of any government. This compilation of work is credited with sparking the ideas for the French Revolution and the concept that the power of royalty was not absolute. It was not something of which the French authority would have approved.

It is difficult to imagine that Voltaire was unaware of this monumental work that was being produced. Was he too involved in his own work? Did he believe he was superior to these young upstarts, even if they were producing the very essence of the Enlightenment? His indifference is difficult to understand.

When the first seven volumes were finally published, however, Voltaire greeted them with enthusiasm, and he immediately became a major contributor. This decision ended his intellectual isolation, and he officially became a leading figure of the Enlightenment. Voltaire appeared to understand, perhaps for the first time, that cooperation among peers was possible—not everyone was a rival.

Voltaire's next three plays were rejected by the Comédie Française. That, and the death of Émilie, made him restless. By this point, he had been corresponding with Frederick the Great of Prussia for more than a decade. Needing a change, Voltaire decided to visit him. Frederick had taken an interest in Enlightenment ideas early on, and he honestly attempted to have peasants and wealthy citizens treated alike in disputes. Frederick also believed that kings derived their power from the people and were answerable to those people. Unsurprisingly, he and Voltaire got along splendidly.

For his visit to the Prussian court in Potsdam, Voltaire needed permission from King Louis XV. He received permission to go, but there was no guarantee that he would be able to return to Paris. Voltaire's stay in Potsdam stretched to three years from 1750 to 1753. During that time, he appeared very depressed, whether due to Émilie's death or fear that he may not be allowed to return home is not certain. Perhaps it dawned on him that he really was not free to come and go as he pleased. There was also an embarrassing incident only months into his stay in Prussia.

Voltaire had made arrangements with a banker named Abraham Hirsch to buy some Saxon bonds at a discount. The purchase of these bonds was against Prussian law, and Hirsch was subsequently arrested. It was a minor incident, and Voltaire pretended he'd been duped, but it was nevertheless seen as an unsavory financial transaction. Frederick was not pleased, and it greatly affected their friendship. After the incident, Voltaire began to see Frederick less often.

It was in Potsdam that Voltaire first learned about the uproar caused by *Encyclopédie*. A second contributor, Jean-Martin de Prades, was deemed heretical, and a warrant was issued for his arrest. De Prades fled to Holland. Voltaire wrote him, offering him a place to stay and a job as one of Frederick's secretaries. Meanwhile, he published *Sermon des Cinquante*, a fiery attack on Christianity. Frederick publicly opposed Voltaire's attacks on religion and became increasingly annoyed by Voltaire's inability to stay out of trouble. Their differences escalated into a public argument, which led to Voltaire spending three weeks under house arrest. In March of 1753, he finally left Frederick's employment.

His travels led him through Frankfurt, where he was briefly reunited with Marie-Louise. He then continued the journey leisurely on his own, still uncertain of the type of welcome he would receive at Versailles after his employment by Frederick in Prussia. By January 1754, Voltaire learned from Madame de Pompadour that Louis XV would not welcome his return. The reality of another exile came as a shock. Even worse, there was no mention of how long he was to be forbidden entry into France.

Without any other options, he settled down in the border city of Colmar, where he was joined by Marie-Louise.

Chapter Six

Years in Exile

"It is dangerous to be right in matters where established men are wrong."

—Voltaire

Still not certain what to do, Voltaire moved to the city-state of Geneva, which would later become part of Switzerland. He and Marie-Louise rented a chateau by Lake Geneva until they could find something more permanent. Marie-Louise busied herself with decorating their new residence and turning it into a home. The property was breathtakingly beautiful with a view of the lake, but it was also unbearably cold in the winter, and Voltaire was soon looking for another place.

By law, Catholics could not own property in Geneva, which had turned into an exile for Huguenots. Being French, Voltaire was automatically considered Catholic. To be able to purchase a house, he and a banker friend, Jean-Robert Tronchin, devised a scheme whereby the new house would be in Tronchin's name while Voltaire provided him with the purchase money. Upon Voltaire's death, ownership of the house, called Les Délices, would revert to Tronchin.

The lifestyle in Calvinist Geneva was austere. The city had turned into a Protestant haven, protected from Rome and France. The rules instituted by Calvin, however, were equally as severe. Citizens were expected to forego luxuries. These same citizens were expected to keep an eye on each other and report any deviant behavior. Church attendance was mandatory. Laws specified the amount of food permitted at each meal and what type of garments were appropriate. No jewelry or rouge was allowed. Gambling, card games, and drinking were forbidden.

It was a strange place for Voltaire to settle, and he didn't waste any time flaunting the rules. He hired many servants, imported luxurious food items, and traveled by magnificent coach and six horses. Unsurprisingly, he managed to immediately irritate the conservative Calvinist population. To add to his crimes, he produced plays in his own home by hiring actors from the Comédie Française. At this time, he also finished his play *The Orphan of China* and had it sent to the Comédie Française for staging. Theater, of course, was forbidden in Geneva.

Voltaire appeared to enjoy irritating the authorities. After Marie-Louise's sister moved in and complained about the lack of bidets (another taboo item in Geneva), he happily ordered three bidets to be delivered. Genevans themselves were divided as to their new resident. Many wished he had settled elsewhere. Others were intrigued by his lifestyle. As to Voltaire, he was having the time of his life in exile. He used this time to contribute many articles to the *Encyclopédie*, which was continuing to cause quite a stir. After d'Alembert visited Geneva to work on articles with Voltaire, he wrote his own piece, *Genève,* detailing his observations. In it, d'Alembert urged Genevans to put an end to their theater-ban, and he attacked their view of harsh

Christianity. Of course, Voltaire was blamed for the debacle.

The elites in Paris were just as incensed. The *Encyclopédie* was viewed, and rightly so, as anti-religion. This caused a huge rift between the court and the contributors to the *Encyclopédie*. Voltaire, comfortably ensconced in his lakeside home, was unaware of the brewing storm. He continued to order more decadent supplies, such as fine sugar, wine, and coffee. When the French court rescinded permission for the *Encyclopédie* to continue publication, d'Alembert withdrew as editor in protest of this censorship. Diderot continued. Reluctantly, Voltaire stopped contributing any articles. He, too, would not abide government censorship.

With most of Geneva in an uproar about *Encyclopédie*, Voltaire decided he needed another place to live. He kept his beloved Les Délices but bought two other homes. By now, he had accepted that his exile from Paris would be permanent. He acquired two properties just outside of Geneva. One was an estate in Ferney; the other was the chateau de Tournay. Both areas had tenants that were overwhelmed by tax burdens, causing them to live lives of misery. Almost immediately following the purchases, Voltaire paid off all taxes for these tenants.

While his philosophy had previous been abstract, he was now seeing concrete proof of the pain caused by governmental power. It was his own ideas brought to life. This realization brought about a change in Voltaire. He now connected his ideas to morality and decided to be on the side of the moral. He hired dozens of people to cultivate his fields and improve the buildings. Before long, the chateau de Tournay had a theater that could hold 100 viewers. People were willing to travel a considerable distance to see one of Voltaire's productions. With the success of his Tournay theater, he built a 300-seat theater at Ferney. Voltaire was nearing the age of 65 and enjoying life.

While still writing his plays, he was about to start another important project, the *Dictionnaire philosophique*, which was published anonymously in 1764. The articles were in alphabetical order, with major emphasis on criticism of various religions. It was the culmination of Voltaire's view on the tyranny and injustices of Christianity. He deliberately made it short and affordable to provide access even to poor people. The *Dictionnaire philosophique* had a mixed reception. It sold out quickly, and many more editions had to be printed. Both Frederick of Prussia and Catherine II of Russian were enthusiastic supporters. But, not surprisingly, it was hated by the religious authorities, who censored its publication in Geneva and France. Copies found in either country were immediately burned.

Chapter Seven

Candide and Morality

"I have no morals, yet I am a very moral person."

—Voltaire

Voltaire's *Candide* stands as a major satire of the Enlightenment. It challenges the idea that optimism, or God, will provide.

Candide is an optimistic young man who lives in an Eden-like paradise. His mentor, Pangloss, has ingrained him with the idea that a just and all-powerful God created the world. As a result, the world and everything that happens must be God's will and perfect. Anything that appears to be wrong is merely a lack of human understanding. Pangloss ignores any evidence to the contrary. In addition to irrational optimism, Pangloss advocates a complacent attitude toward evil and wrongdoing. If it is God's will, why argue? As an example, when Pangloss's friend is struggling in the bay of Lisbon, Pangloss keeps Candide from rescuing his friend from drowning. He states that the bay of Lisbon must have been specifically created to achieve this particular drowning.

In *Candide*, Voltaire deliberately ridicules fanaticism and religion. While the book was successful, it was considered scandalous and banned in many places because of its religious blasphemy. Since its publication in 1759,

Candide is considered one of the 100 most influential books written. While the tone of *Candide* is light and amusing, its criticism of religion is brutal, and the book remained banned in the United States until the early twentieth century.

One major criticism of *Candide* is that the character finds no alternative answers after rejecting his irrational optimism. The reason for this is that Voltaire himself, although an opponent of organized religion, was a Deist. He struggled with the question of how to incorporate a rational God in an irrational world without finding a solution. Other, more minor, themes run through *Candide*. One of them is the supposed superiority of the rich and elite. Voltaire had always hated the pretensions of the upper classes. In his youth, he paid the price for his dislike with imprisonments at the Bastille, and his attitude had not changed with age. In *Candide*, he presents Candide's mother as a snobbish aristocrat who looks down on Candide's father merely because he is a lesser noble.

There are a number of good Samaritans in the novel. Their presence reveals the kindness of which people are capable when left to their own devices without having their behavior forced by governments or churches. Voltaire had been defiant of authority, governmental or religious, all his life. As a young man, he'd happily thumped his nose at social superiors for the sheer pleasure of doing so. With advancing age, however, he saw that defiance on its own did not constitute morality. If there was no authority to guide a person's behavior, then obviously, the person had to be responsible for his or her deeds, whether right or wrong. Morality, he concluded, was the result of taking responsible action instead of blindly obeying those in power.

Following the publication of *Candide*, Voltaire's life was content. He enjoyed his homes, and he and Marie-Louise entertained frequently. At the age of 65, Voltaire tired easily and went to bed early, but it pleased him that while he rested, Marie-Louise was entertaining royalty and other prominent people. Then, in 1760, fate brought a major change to his life.

Through an acquaintance, he learned of a teenage girl in Paris whose father was barely able to support her. Her name was Marie-Françoise Corneille, a descendant of the seventeenth-century dramatist Pierre Corneille. Voltaire immediately invited her to stay with him and Marie-Louise. When Marie-Françoise arrived, they welcomed her as a surrogate daughter. Voltaire took great delight in his new role as a father. She showed some acting talent, and Voltaire provided her with a few small parts in his plays.

The crucial thing, however, was to find Marie-Françoise a husband. This would require a dowry. To get the needed funds, Voltaire suggested to the Comédie Française that he would write an endorsement and commentary of Pierre Corneille's plays. The Comédie Française agreed to the project. It turned out that many of Pierre Corneille's plays were not to Voltaire's liking, and he ended up denouncing them. Still, the book, which was published in a beautiful deluxe edition, was a success, and Marie-Françoise received 40,000 pounds.

Voltaire and Marie-Louise arranged for the marriage of their adopted daughter in 1763. The suitable candidate was Pierre-Jacques-Claude de la Chaux. Voltaire already knew the young man and considered it a suitable match. Luckily, Marie-Françoise and Pierre-Jacques fell passionately in love upon being introduced. The wedding was held at Voltaire's home. Since neither of them had any family, Voltaire invited them to live with him. He was getting older, still enjoying his relationship with Marie-Louise, and now added fatherhood to his pleasures.

At the same time, a horrible legal case brought out the social warrior in Voltaire. It began on October 13, 1761 when the son of Huguenot merchant Jean Calas was found dead. The family insisted that the young man, Marc-Antoine, had been murdered. In France, a very Catholic country, the death of a Protestant Huguenot did not warrant further inquiry. The dead man, Marc-Antoine, had studied for his law degree, and in order to practice law, it was necessary for him to convert to Catholicism. He had refused. This, of course, was very suspicious to the Catholic Church. The authorities looked to blame the Calas family for Marc-Antoine's death, claiming that they had killed him to prevent his conversion to Catholicism.

The case became of the talk of France. The family was arrested with the issuance of proper warrants. Jean Calas, the father, was eventually tortured to get him to confess. When he did not, he was executed. Although Voltaire was still banished from Paris during this event, he received news of it in Geneva. His first reaction was a brutal quip, reminiscent of the youthful snide sarcasm that had landed him in the Bastille. "We may not be worth much, but the Huguenots are worse." Yet in the days and weeks to come, as Voltaire learned more about the case, his mood shifted from condescension to concern to outrage. In 1762, he began a three-year campaign to bring justice to the Calas family. He provided the widow Calas with funds to appeal the case. He anonymously wrote legal documents, spoke with the best lawyers, and called upon his aristocratic friends for support. He was livid at the French judiciary system which permitted the court to keep evidence secret.

One official ordered Voltaire to step back: "Let the world wag its own way." Voltaire ignored him. In 1763, he wrote about the case in a work called *Treatise on Tolerance*, which argued vehemently for religious tolerance. *Treatise on Tolerance* caused havoc within both the French government and the church. The postal system in Geneva refused to mail any copies and destroyed any they could get a hold of. Opening mail was standard procedure in Geneva. Still, in 1764, thanks to Voltaire's efforts, the Calas case was reopened. By the following year, the father was found innocent of any wrongdoing. Although they had already executed Jean Calas, the new verdict at least restored the man's reputation and the family also received 36,000 livres by King Louis XV in compensation. The original prosecutor who had found him guilty committed suicide.

Although Voltaire's health was in decline, the Calas case convinced him to continue being involved in cases of injustice. He was compelled to see his words turned into concrete action. Otherwise, what would be their meaning? At the age of 71, he felt the need to not just write about justice, but to actively work for it.

Chapter Eight

Voltaire and the French Legal System

"Men are equal; it is not birth, it is virtue alone that makes them differ."

—Voltaire

By 1765, Voltaire was growing frailer. He still enjoyed putting on plays in his private theaters and even added bedrooms to his house at Ferney to accommodate the frequent overnight guests. He no longer had the strength to spend much time with them, but Marie-Louise was a superb hostess.

At this time, Voltaire developed an intense interest in the French legal system. The problem was, there was no such thing as equality under the law. Crimes against members of the aristocracy were punished far more severely than similar crimes against commoners. There were laws that commoners had to obey, but the aristocracy and the church did not. Even trivial crimes could receive the death penalty. Torture to elicit a confession was perfectly acceptable and legal. Previous Enlightenment thinkers, such as Locke, had criticized the French legal system. Now, Voltaire felt compelled to take up the cause.

Voltaire eagerly read a book called *On Crimes and Punishments* written by an Italian nobleman called Cesare Beccaria. Beccaria was a member of the Italian Enlightenment movement in Milan and first and foremost raged against legalized torture and the death penalty. *On Crimes and Punishments* was a landmark publication on criminal reform and penology. It reflected the thinking of French Enlightenment judge Montesquieu, who wrote that "every punishment which does not arise from absolute necessity is tyrannical." These words spoke deeply to Voltaire. In this Age of Reason, Beccaria was arguing for reasonable and fair laws, and Voltaire could not have agreed more fervently.

Of course, the book was heavily criticized by the Catholic Church, which would have only heightened Voltaire's interest. He helped and encouraged his old friend d'Alembert to arrange for a French translation. This translation was even more popular than the Italian original. As a complement to the book, Voltaire wrote a commentary which was published both separately and as part of the original book. Most of his commentary focused on the barbarism which existed in the French legal system. Although Voltaire was still living in Geneva, the irritated French Prime Minister wrote to him, "Why in the devil's name are you agitating so much, you Swiss marmot?" Even in his old age, Voltaire knew how to get under the skin of authority figures.

Another legal case that Voltaire became involved in was that of Thomas Lally. Lally was a French general and confirmed Jacobite. He lost the vital Battle of Wandiwash to the British during the Seven Years' War, and the defeat of the French army was blamed on him. After spending time in Britain as a prisoner of war, Lally voluntarily returned to France to stand trial. He remained a prisoner in France for two years. When his case finally went to trial, Lally was not informed of the charges against him, nor was he allowed an attorney. Although the charges were never made clear, he was pronounced guilty and sentenced to death for the crime of treason. He was publicly executed in 1766. All of this was standard practice under the French legal system.

Voltaire was familiar with Lally, although he didn't particularly like him. He knew Lally had a hot temper. To a friend, he wrote, "I knew Lally-Tollendal for an absurd man, violent, ambitious, capable of pillage and abuse of power; but I should be astonished if he was a traitor." Gérard de Lally-Tollendal, Lally's son, asked Voltaire for help in 1770 in an effort to restore his father's good name. The relevant documents had been held secret during the original trial, and no reason had ever been given for the treason charges. This was perfectly legal in a French court. The very arbitrariness of this system infuriated Voltaire. King Louis XV refused to become involved and blamed his ministers. The records did indicate that even if Lally didn't commit treason, the harm he caused in losing a battle was cause enough to condemn him to death. No other explanation or reason was given. With Voltaire's help, the son was permitted to appeal the case, and Lally's sentence would eventually be overturned.

Due to continued harassment from the Geneva authorities, Voltaire decided to sell Lés Delices and make Ferney his primary home in the mid-1760s. The Petit

Conseil in Geneva was banning his work, as well as the writing of Rousseau. The oligarchs and old-time bourgeois held most of the power in Geneva, while artisans and lower-class citizens held none. While Voltaire insisted publicly that he was not taking sides, his allegiance was with the lower-class citizens, who were about to stage an uprising against the existing class system. They called themselves the Représentants.

During this political upheaval, Voltaire faced another problem. Due to severe French censorship laws, many forbidden books were being smuggled into France from Geneva. One of these smugglers was Madame Lejeune, the wife of a Parisian bookseller. Much of Voltaire's banned work could be found in their shop. To help Madame Lejeune out of Geneva with her load of contraband books, Voltaire lent her Marie-Louise's carriage and horses to carry three trunks of books. A customs inspector named Jeannin was enlisted to help Madame Lejeune across the border. Jeannin, however, betrayed her to the French authorities. Her trunks were opened to reveal the forbidden books, including Voltaire's *Dictionnaire philosophique.*

Voltaire boldly claimed her innocence to the French authorities, indicating Madame Lejeune had no idea of what she had been carrying. Unfortunately, a note from her husband was found. It specified which books Voltaire wanted her to buy and bring across the border. Voltaire's fears worsened when he heard the case might come before the French court. Luck was on his side when the matter was quietly withdrawn.

In the meantime, the class war in Geneva became worse. The French army surrounded the area, preventing food supplies from reaching its citizens. Life became difficult for everyone, even after the troops left the following spring. A temporary truce had been reached stipulating that there would no longer be arbitrary arrests, and artisans and the lower classes were given greater representation in government. The question was, how long would this truce last?

Chapter Nine

Voltaire's Final Years and Death

"I die adoring God, loving my friends, not hating my enemies, and detesting superstition."

—Voltaire

After many years together, Marie-Louise left Voltaire and returned to her home in Paris. The exact reason is unknown, but they had a virulent argument just before her departure from Ferney. The cause may have had to do with the fact Voltaire suspected Marie-Louise was carrying on an illicit relationship with one of his protégés, Jean-François de la Harpe. Voltaire was distraught when she left without saying good-bye. Still, friends believed that he hoped the separation would become permanent. He was tired and wanted to live alone, without the constant socializing Marie-Louise loved. In their view, Voltaire was actually more upset that Marie-Louise had taken their adopted daughter, Marie-Françoise, and her husband with her.

Voltaire continued to correspond with Marie-Louise and helped her out financially. After some hesitation, he even offered to sell Ferney and send her the proceeds. Their ambivalence regarding the sale of their mutual home reflected the ambivalence of their relationship at that point. Neither knew whether to remain apart or to patch things up. Marie-Françoise and her husband returned to Ferney after some time. After months of further negotiation, so did Marie-Louise. Voltaire had his family back.

Meanwhile, the two-year-old truce between the various classes in Geneva became strained when the upper classes simply revoked all the rights previously granted to the lower caste. The lower classes were desperate to flee to France, but the aristocrats asked that the French government forbid them entry. Voltaire commiserated with their plight. As had become his habit, he decided that genuine action was called for. Since there were so many skilled watchmakers in Geneva, he suggested that these skilled laborers settle on his property, Ferney, and devote themselves to creating their own industry. Voltaire was 76 years old and knew nothing about watches, but he liked the idea of helping those persecuted by the authorities.

By April of 1770, Voltaire had a working watch industry thriving on his property. He was entirely involved in the project, ordering gold and other necessary material, as well as cases of wine for the watchmakers. With the increase in population at Ferney, the area needed more merchants to support everyone, so Voltaire arranged to erect buildings at Ferney for them to do business. The watches produced at Ferney were soon marketed around the world. Voltaire even arranged for a sales representative in Paris. He may not be welcome there, but his watches sold extremely well. Little did he know that sales of watches at Ferney would reach half a million pound a year. It was the beginning of the famed Swiss watch industry, which is still held in the highest regard today.

Following the death of King Louis XV in 1774, Voltaire hoped that he might be able to travel to Paris, which he had not seen in decades. He was to be sorely disappointed. The new king, Louis XVI, immediately mandated that upon Voltaire's death, all his manuscripts would be confiscated.

In 1778, Voltaire arranged to enter Paris and visit his beloved Comédie Française, even without permission from the proper authorities. He stayed at the Hotel Villette, where he hosted old friends. The American statesman Benjamin Franklin was one of his admirers and visitors. In March, he was able to attend a performance of his latest play, *Irène*. By the beginning of May, however, Voltaire developed a fever. Religious leaders appeared at his bedside demanding he accept Jesus Christ. Irate and weak, he told them, "In the name of God, do not speak to me about that man, and let me die in peace."

Voltaire died on May 30, 1778, aged 83. With his dying breath, he refused to bow to the pressures of the Catholic Church he so despised. Because of his anti-Catholic views, Voltaire was afraid he would be denied a proper burial. Just a few weeks before his death, he wrote to the Count and Countess of Rochefort asking them to arrange a Christian burial. His fears were not without reason since he had spent his entire life antagonizing the church. Following his death, Voltaire was quickly taken to the Abbey of Scellières in Champagne, just a few hours before the local bishop in Paris attempted to ban such a burial.

After 13 years, Voltaire's body was removed from the Abbey of Scellières and reburied in the Panthéon in Paris. He had been forbidden to enter the city during a large portion of his life, but the French Revolution changed his reputation from a pariah to a national hero. Now, Voltaire was given credit as the inspiration for the people's demand for equality and uprising against the king and queen. His return to Paris was greeted with tremendous fanfare.

While it is ironic that Voltaire's final remains ended up in a church, the Parisian Panthéon is a burial place for the country's national heroes, which Voltaire had become. He certainly earned his place. Voltaire shares his burial site with another social justice warrior, Victor Hugo, and his fellow Enlightenment thinker, Rousseau. Alexander Dumas and scientist Marie Curie are buried within the Panthéon as well.

Conclusion

Voltaire leaves an immense legacy. His advocacy for political, legal, and religious reform is enjoyed in most countries today and considered normal. Many people are entirely unaware of their great debt to Enlightenment thinkers. Voltaire fought for religious freedom and the right to worship as one pleases. That, too, has become the norm around the world. During his own time, it was a radical idea which led to the banning of his books and a lifetime of battle with the Catholic Church.

Voltaire's ideas greatly influenced the French Revolution. No revolution is possible without a set of ideas. Although Voltaire was not the most revolutionary of the Enlightenment thinkers, he was one of the most prolific. Even when his work was banned, many people read his books, plays, and essay. Voltaire's ideas prepared ordinary citizens to challenge the absolute rule of kings, which they had accepted for so long. Voltaire told the French people that kings did not have God-given rights, and when they stormed the Bastille in 1789, they believed him.

The world that Voltaire envisioned, and worked hard to achieve, was a world of justice, where every person was born equal. For the creators of the Constitution of the United States of America, Voltaire opened their eyes to the injustices inflicted by a cruel government and the importance of liberty. The founders of America based their country upon these ideas.

Except for his novel *Candide,* not much of Voltaire's work is read in modern times. Still, his ideas prevail. He is best known for his plea for tolerance of ideas. Evelyn Beatrice Hall's summary of Voltaire's beliefs, "I may disapprove of what you say, but I will defend to the death your right to say it," lives on and is still widely quoted today.

Some critics have pointed out that while Voltaire was preaching tolerance, he was extremely intolerant of government inequality and the Catholic Church. His writings are essentially filled with intolerance. That is, however, not much of a contradiction. Voltaire had no difficulty in accepting different ideas. It was the implementation of unjust ideas that he objected to. He didn't mind the existence of the Catholic Church. What he fought against was the church's insistence on preventing its followers from asking questions and arriving at their own conclusion. All he asked was that people be allowed to challenge their own thinking. In that, Voltaire was very successful.

CPSIA information can be obtained
at www.ICGtesting.com
Printed in the USA
LVHW052141071019
633407LV00005B/2043/P

9 781693 489525